Quintessential

Choir

A Comprehensive Choral Method

Church Choir Edition

Quintessential Choir

A Comprehensive Choral Method

Church Choir Edition

Nicholas C. Breiner

To the Reader

As a member of the music ministry in your church, you are taking part in an age old tradition as given to the Levites:

"David also commanded the chiefs of the Levites to appoint their kindred as the singers to play on musical instruments, on harps and lyres and cymbals, to raise loud sounds of joy." (1 Chronicles 15:16)

This text is designed to help you along the way. Contained within are the basics of proper vocal technique, music reading, and the history of your tradition as well as sight reading and performance exercises to help you hone your skill. Welcome to choir. Now, go and make a joyful noise.

First Printing: 2014

ISBN: 978-0-578-13699-8

Monticello Press
122 Ronameki Dr.
Mount Sterling, KY 40353

For Susan
Without you, I may never have directed a choir

Contents

Acknowledgements

I would like to thank my teachers, my parents, my friends, and everyone who has helped me get to where I am now. I would also like to give a very special thanks to:

Fr. Frank Brawner, Pastor of St. Patrick's Church in Mt. Sterling, KY, and St. Joseph's Church in Winchester, KY.

Dr. Greg Detweiler, Associate Professor of Choirs & Conducting, Director of Choral Activities, Morehead State University. Choir Director at First Baptist Church, Morehead, KY.

John Stegner, retired public school choral director of 34 years, Director of Music at First Christian Church in Richmond, KY, Director of Choirs at Bluegrass Community and Technical College in Lexington, KY, and Adjunct Instructor of Choral Methods at University of the Cumberlands in Williamsburg, KY.

Ashley Tyree, Choir Director at Montgomery Co. High School in Mt. Sterling, KY. Choir Director at First Christian Church, Mt. Sterling, KY.

Foreword

Mr. Nicholas Breiner, an accomplished singer and choir director for Saint Patrick's Catholic Church in Mount Sterling, Kentucky has been involved with the education and preparation for meaningful and worshipful liturgies for his parish for several years. Bringing his skills and talents to a small, poor parish with few musical resources, Mr. Breiner has grown both the choir and the quality of worship in the church where he serves. He bears tremendous talents in both vocal work and music education and these have seen the flourishing of St. Patrick's, with Christmas and Easter liturgies that draw attention and inspire.

St. Augustine reminds us, "he who sings prays twice," and so a mission of the Church to *pray unceasingly* as Saint Paul exhorts, is most befitting engaged when a parish develops and utilizes a well-trained choir. In this book, Mr. Breiner provides his insights into the training and formation of a choir so as to make not only a *joyful noise to the Lord*, but a beautiful one as well. His method, employed at Saint Patrick's, provides an easy and practical help for any choir member or director, grounding the choir in those basics which even the most well-trained might forget.

Mr. Breiner provides in this work a simple, coherent and much needed text to foster and support our choirs, which work so diligently to offer a melodious gift to God. The work reflects his own indomitable passion for education, music and worship, and his gifts for bringing the benefits of formal musical training into the hands and mouths eager and thankful volunteers. *Quintessential Choir* provides an invaluable resource to choirs and parishes who look to improve the choral training, or even to begin a choir for the very first time. As a Pastor, and as one who appreciates the beauty of the Church's rich musical heritage, I am thankful and indebted to Mr. Breiner and his work.

Rev. Fr. Frank Brawner
Pastor

Introduction

Welcome to the *Quintessential Choir* series. You will notice, as you progress through this book, that *Quintessential Choir* is a method organized around five aspects of music education. These five aspects are:

- Vocal Technique
- Music Theory
- Music History
- Sight-Reading
- Performance

Each chapter is designed to be a progression of each of these five aspects in succession in order to give you, the reader, a more well-rounded foundation of musical knowledge and skills on which to stand as you grow as a musician.

As you progress through the book, you will often be asked to try an example or demonstrate a principle. Don't skip this step! Reading the book is a good first step, but to truly aim towards mastery of the material, you need to transfer the knowledge of this book into real life and apply the principles it contains to your own music making. As the jazz legend, Thelonious Monk once said, "writing about music is like dancing about architecture." You have to get out there and do it!

Welcome to *Quintessential Choir* and happy learning!

Chapter 1

Technique: Posture

"Stand up straight!" How many times have you heard that in your life? Try it. You can certainly do it. Straighten your back and stand as tall as possible. I'm sure that you look great. Now try to sing like that. How uncomfortable are you? Extremely? I'll bet. Now relax and let me let you in on a little trade secret. Everything we do in proper vocal technique is to allow ourselves to be lazy. If you feel like you're working too hard when you sing, you probably are. Have you ever seen a picture of a spine? It has a natural curve to it. To straighten it out is to do something completely unnatural (and more than a little uncomfortable). When we sing, we should maintain this natural curve by "standing tall," NOT straight or rigid. What do I mean by that? Well here's a checklist from your feet up.

Posture While Standing

- **Feet** should be placed shoulder width apart with one foot slightly in front of the other
- **Knees** should stay relaxed. Don't lock them or you might faint.
- **Back** should stand tall, but not straight or rigid.
- **Rib cage** should stay high or "lifted."
- **Shoulders** should be relaxed and sloped naturally.
- Your **head** should float from the top center of your head to the ceiling.

Technique: Breathing

Take a big deep breath. Did your shoulders rise up? If they did, then you are allowing your shoulders to constrict your air flow (making it harder on yourself). The most perfect breath you will find in nature is that of a newborn baby. They breathe what we call "diaphragmatically." It's a five dollar word for a five cent concept, and it's really simple. Have you ever seen professional wrestling? Even if you haven't, I imagine you are familiar with the championship belt. Breathe again but, this time, imagine that you're wearing that belt. This is your championship breathing belt. Feel where it would lie across your middle. As you breathe, make it your aim to expand that belt outward. Another way of thinking about is like filling a glass of water. You fill it *from the bottom up*. Your lungs are no different. Take a second and try it. Make sure you keep your shoulders relaxed and just let the air fall into your lungs. They will rise a little, but make sure you're not actively doing it. Just let the air do it.

Music Theory: Notes and Rests

Learning to read music is not unlike learning another language. Similarly to learning a language, to learn to read music, we need to learn what all of the symbols mean. It's like the musical equivalent of the alphabet. Let's start with the most basic symbols that you will need to know. Let's learn about notes and rests.

Notes

Simply put, a note is just a symbol that indicates how long a pitch should be played or sung. The longest of these (that you need to worry about for now) is the whole note (o). Typically, whole notes receive 4 beats. If you then take that whole note and break it up into two even notes, you're left with two half notes (♩ ♩). A half note typically receives 2 beats (notice that 2 is exactly half of 4). If we then take each of those half notes and divide each of them into even notes, we're left with 4 quarter notes (♩ ♩ ♩ ♩). A quarter note typically receives 1 beat. We can repeat this process for 8th and 16th notes that get ½ and ¼ beat respectively. Here is a chart to help you visualize it:

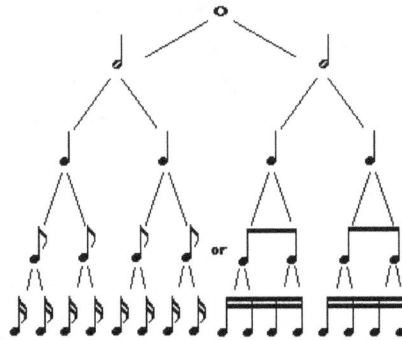

Rests

Rests are the other basic symbol type that you will need to get started. Like notes, rests are a measure of duration. However, rests are a measure of the duration of silence instead of sound. Rests use different symbols, but they use the same names and break down the same way. Check it out below:

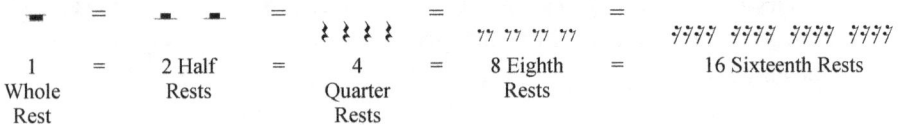

1 Whole Rest	=	2 Half Rests	=	4 Quarter Rests	=	8 Eighth Rests	=	16 Sixteenth Rests

Music History: Early Christian Music

The earliest Christian Church, of course, was simply a sect within the context of Judaism. Thus, in that time period, Christian music history runs concurrently with its Jewish roots. In those days, the two faiths were remarkably similar and it was typical that Christians still attended synagogues and the Temple in Jerusalem as Christ had done.

Of course, the earliest known use of music in religious ritual is attributed to King David. The Bible credits David with charging the Levites with the sacred duty of being custodians of sacred music.

"David also commanded the chiefs of the Levites to appoint their kindred as the singers to play on musical instruments, on harps and lyres and cymbals, to raise loud sounds of joy."

1 Chronicles 15:16

David Playing the Harp by Jan de Bray, 1670

Ultimately, the 150 Psalms attributed to David became the cornerstone for early Biblical music. There are a number of further mentions of the use of music in the Bible, including in the Gospel of Matthew, just before the Crucifixion.

"When they had sung a hymn, they went out into the Mount of Olives."

Matthew 26:30

But what did it sound like?

Unfortunately, very few records exist on music history in ancient times. This is primarily due to music notation being very much in its infancy. As a result, music was often passed down in the same way as history; via an oral tradition.

We do know that, while David charged the Levites with the use of musical instruments, use of musical instruments in the early Christian Church seems to have been discouraged. It is believed that this is due to an apparent association of musical instruments with pagan rites, and the need to separate from the pagan faiths. St. Jerome is even quoted as having said "A Christian maiden ought not even to know what a lyre or a flute is, or what it is used for." Thus, it may be presumed that the earliest music in the Christian Church was primarily a vocal tradition.

It was not until the 7th century, during the papacy of Pope Vitalian, that church organ music began to become the norm. And it was, from that point, that the Church would become a driving force in the development of music for centuries to come.

Sight-Reading: Rhythm

While clapping a steady beat, count aloud the following rhythmic patterns using the syllables listed below each note. HINT – If you're having trouble counting through the rests, try saying "rest" on each beat/clap that you rest.

1.

2.

3.

4.

5.

6.

7.

8.

9.

10.

HINT – Half notes giving you trouble? Don't fret. Even at the professional level, half notes are often the most misinterpreted rhythm. We tend to either make them too long or too short, depending on the tempo. Remember that half notes get two beats. It may help you in your counting to give an extra vocal "pulse" to the second beat. Instead of a steady "Ta," it would sound like "Ta-ah." Try it!

Performance: *Be Thou My Vision*

Be Thou My Vision, originally titled *Bí Thusa 'mo Shúile,* is a traditional hymn from Ireland, attributed to St. Dallán Forgaill (ca. 530-598). It is one of the earliest known examples of Christian hymns and remains popular today. The music itself comes from the Irish folk song, *Slane*. Notice that the time signature is ¾, indicating that each measure is three beats long instead of four. Your counting, however, is the same.

Be Thou my Vi-sion, O Lord of my heart; Naught be all else to me, save that Thou

art Thou my best Thought - by day or by night,

Wak - ing or sleep - ing Thy pres - ence my light.

NOTE
- You'll notice that *Be Thou My Vision* makes use of eighth notes. To count them, simply use the syllables "Ti-ki" to count pairs of eighth notes. Remember there are two eighth notes in a beat. Thus, to count the first measure, you would say "Ta – Ta – Ti-ki."
- Dotted half notes (like the one in measure 4) get 3 beats each. To count them, simply count them like a half note and add another beat. Thus, counting a dotted half note would sound like this: "Ta-ah-ah." Try it!

TIP
- Notice that *Be Thou My Vision* does not make use of rests. Typically, we try to take breaths on rests whenever possible but, here, you have no such option. In the absence of a rest, try saving breaths for punctuation in the text. As a general rule, it is acceptable to breathe on a comma in the text. DO NOT breathe in the middle of a word. Plan out your breaths as much as possible and mark them in your music ahead of time so that you don't have to think about them. See chapter 5 for more information on score marking.

Chapter 2

Technique: The 5 Latin Vowels – 5 Keys to Tone

When a vowel is pronounced, air may flow freely and even continuously from the lungs through the oral cavity without any significant obstruction by any oral components. Not all vowels are created equally, however, and there are a few that we favor in vocal music as being less obstructive. These are the 5 Latin Vowels, taken primarily from the Classical Method of Latin pronunciation. The more open the oral cavity is allowed to be; the easier it is to create a full rich vocal tone. Again, everything we do in vocal technique is to make it easier on ourselves. The 5 Latin Vowels are as follows:

ā   Pronounced "ah" as in father.
ē   Pronounced "eh" as in feather.
ī   Pronounced "ee" as in sheep.
ō   Pronounced "oh" as in holy.
ū   Pronounced "oo" as in root.

The 5 Latin Vowels are by no means an exhaustive list of the vowel shapes available to us, but they are a good place to start as a "go to" resource when deciding how to pronounce a word. Ultimately, the pronunciation decision goes to the director, of course.

TIP – *The Soft Palette*

The idea with the use of these vowel shapes is to allow for the most open and unobstructed oral cavity as possible. To achieve this desired sound, it is important to make our oral shape *tall* instead of wide. A wide vowel shape will lead to a bright and even nasal sound. This is a sound that is not uncommon in American speech, but it is not the most pleasant sound in vocal music. Instead, opt for a *taller* shape. This is achieved by raising the soft palette. Don't know what your soft palette is? Don't worry, most people don't. Take your tongue and run it along the roof of your mouth. Feel the hard ridged bit behind your teeth? That's called the *hard* palette. If you run your tongue back further, you will come to a soft fleshy bit that will give when you push up into it. That is the soft palette. Now, how to you raise that? Easy. Yawn. When you yawn, you automatically raise the soft palette. This is so there is as little obstruction to the airflow as possible (the exact same reason we do this when we sing). Now, once you stop yawning (sorry, I know how contagious it is), imagine that you have just taken a bite of extremely hot food. If you didn't immediately spit it out, you probably raised your soft palette and perhaps even made a couple of "hoh" shaped short breaths. Congratulations. You just mastered the use of your soft palette. Now try practicing with its use as you sing.

Music Theory: The Grand Staff

Now that we've learned notes and rests, it's time to find out where and how we place them on the grand staff. First off, what's a grand staff? The piano's grand staff is a system of two staves consisting of a treble staff on top and a bass staff on the bottom. These staves are connected by a brace and by barlines throughout the music. Take a look at the figure below:

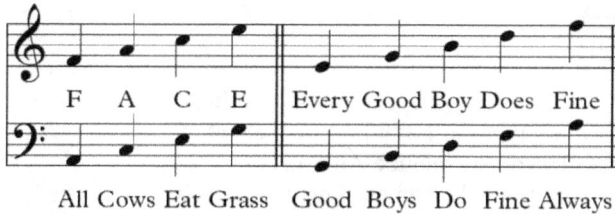

These are some common mnemonic devices we use to remember what pitch each space and line on the staff indicates. Here is the completed staff:

The letter underneath each note indicates the pitch name for the corresponding line or space on the grand staff. Notice how the treble and bass staves overlap at the pitch "C" in the middle. That "C" is called "middle C." It is also the pitch at the very center of a standard 88 key piano.

Typically, if you are singing the Soprano or Alto parts, you will be singing a *treble* clef line and will use the same pitches indicated on the upper half of the grand staff. If you sing the Bass part, you will read a *bass* clef staff, or the lower half of the grand staff. If you sing the tenor part, some music will also be written in bass clef, but you may also see a clef that looks like this:

This is called the Suboctave Treble Clef. A fair amount of tenor parts are written using this. Don't be intimidated by the cool name. It reads exactly the same as the regular treble clef. The "suboctave" bit (indicated by the 8 on the bottom of the treble clef) simply indicates that the pitch will *sound* an octave (a musical interval of eight tones) lower than written, which is typical of a fully developed male voice in comparison to a female voice.

7

Music History: Gregorian Chant

Traditionally, the invention of Gregorian chant is attributed to Pope St. Gregory the Great. This is disputed by some scholars who believe that it arose from a later synthesis of Roman chant and Gallican chant. Regardless of its origin, it cannot be disputed that Gregorian chant became a driving force in the development of western music; particularly through the 9th and 10th centuries. Well beyond that, for about a millennium, Gregorian chant was still commonplace within the context of Catholicism until the Second Vatican Council (1962-1965).

Gregorian chant is, of course, a vocal music tradition. It is one of five primary types of Latin liturgical chant of the Middle Ages. The others include Ambrosian, Gallican, Mozarabic, and Old Roman. The music itself consists of unaccompanied melodies set to Latin texts of the liturgy. Thus, the major driving force in western musical development of the time was sacred, whereas from the Renaissance through today, it is primarily secular.

Pope Gregory I dictating the Gregorian chants (ca. 1000)

Gregorian chant began as a monastic tradition. Monks sang the "Divine Service" at nine times throughout the day. Singing psalms was a large part of life in the monastic community and remains so today, though many chants are not necessarily done in Latin anymore.

Through the centuries, the evolution of Gregorian chant led to the development of polyphony (music that combines several distinct melodic lines simultaneously) through the works of composers such as Léonin and Pérotin. Though this innovation is certainly commonplace today, it was a revolutionary concept in western music at the time, and paved the way for all of the musical developments to come.

The development of Gregorian chant even led to the development of modern music notation. Where once, music notation was as simple as a roughly drawn line to indicate the relative rise and fall of pitch, absent entirely of rhythm, the development of neumatic notation (seen in the figure to the right) created music that is nearly like music we have today. Compare that to one of the earliest forms of music notation as seen in The Seikilos epitaph (ca. 1st century), seen below:

C Z̄ Z̄ KIZĪ   K̄ I Ż ĪK O C̄ O̅Φ̅
Ὁ σον ζῆς φαί νου   μη δὲν ὅ λως σὺ λυ ποῦ
C KZ I K̇IKC̄ O̅Φ̅   C KO I Ż K̇ C C̄ CX̅I
πρὸς ὁ λί γον ἐσ τὶ τὸ ζῆν   τὸ τέ λος ὁ χρό νος ἀπ αι τεῖ.

8

Sight-Reading: Solfège

Perhaps you have, in the past, heard a singer singing in some seemingly nonsensical language. Perhaps your first exposure was through the homonymic ramblings of Julie Andrews in The Sound of Music. When a singer sight-reads a piece of music, or sings a scale, rarely do they use actual words or pitch names but, instead, opt to use a system called solfège, whereby each pitch of the scale is given a different syllable.

The principle behind the system is to create a psychological muscle memory for developing relative pitch. Just like any athlete, magician, or professional acrobatic cat burglar, muscle memory is critical to ensure accuracy.

Solfège very simply puts syllables in place to stand in for each member of a scale. Try singing up and down the C Major scale below, using solfège syllables.

Do Re Mi Fa Sol La Ti Do

For now, we're going to just concentrate on the first three scale degrees; Do (pronounced "doh"), Re (pronounced "ray"), and Mi (pronounced "mee"). Try the examples below:

1.

Do Re Do Re Do   Do Re Mi Re Do

2.

Do   Re   Do Re Do Do   Do Re Mi Re Do

3.

Do   Re   Do Re Do Do   Do Re Mi Re Do

4.

Do Re Do Re Mi Do Re Do Do Mi Re Do Mi Re Do

5.

Try writing in the solfège for this example on your own!

9

Performance: All Creatures of Our God and King

First known as *Laudes Creaturarum* (Praise of the Creatures), The text for *All Creatures of Our God and King* is said to have been primarily composed by St. Francis of Assisi in late 1224 while recovering from an illness at San Damiano. A legend states that the piece was not physically written by him due to his blindness but, instead, dictated as St. Francis "looked at nature through the eye of mind." The text was translated into English by William H. Draper in 1919 and set to the 17th century German hymn *Lasst Uns Erfreuen.*

All Crea-tures of our God and King Lift up your voice and with us sing, Al-le - lu - ia! Al-le

lu - ia! Thou burn-ing sun with gold-en beam, Thou sil-ver moon with soft-er gleam! O___

praise Him! O___ praise Him! Al-le - lu - ia! Al-le - lu - ia! Al-le - lu - ia!

NOTE

- You'll notice that (like *Be Thou My Vision*) *All Creatures of Our God and King* makes use of eighth notes. Recall from chapter one, to count them, simply use the syllables "Ti-ki" to count pairs of eighth notes. Remember there are two eighth notes in a beat. Thus, to count the first measure, you would say "Ta – Ta – Ti-ki."
- Remember, dotted half notes (like the one in last measure) get 3 beats each. To count them, simply count them like a half note and add another beat. Thus, counting a dotted half note would sound like this: "Ta-ah-ah." Try it!

TIP

- Notice that *All Creatures of Our God and King* does not make use of rests (except for before the first note and after the last). Typically, we try to take breaths on rests whenever possible but, here, you have no such option. In the absence of a rest, try saving breaths for punctuation in the text. As a general rule, it is acceptable to breathe on a comma in the text. DO NOT breathe in the middle of a word. Plan out your breaths as much as possible and mark them in your music ahead of time so that you don't have to think about them. See chapter 5 for more information on score marking.

Chapter 3

Technique: Breath Support

The voice is, essentially, a wind instrument. It requires air to function. In this way, your voice is no different from a clarinet or tuba. It should then come as no surprise that the most important aspect of our vocal sound is how we use our breath.

By now you should be getting an idea of what proper posture is (as in, posture that allows for the freest flowing of air), and what this "championship breathing belt" thing is all about. If not, that's okay. Keep going back to the previous chapters and practice it. Breathing for musicians is not as simple a concept as it would seem on its surface. I could fill an entire book with information just about breathing (and some people have). Keep at it and it'll start to make sense.

When you sing, the vocal folds contained within your larynx (voice box) close and begin to vibrate under the pressure of air being expelled from your lungs. Vocal tone, then, is simply the manipulation of the tension of those vocal folds combined with the control of air pressure. This control of air pressure is called breath support.

Often when trying to sing in the high range or at a louder dynamic level, less experienced singers will try to place extra tension in the throat in order to "muscle it out." This might instill you with the heroic feeling of the little engine that could, but it should not be your aim as a vocalist. Remember that excess tension in your body will translate into tension in your sound. You might feel like a hero, but you likely sound something like a dying cat and your vocal endurance will be severely impacted. Instead, muscular support for singing and breath support should be across your middle. The "championship belt muscles," if you will. We don't want to use the word "tension." Tension is a bad word among musicians. Instead, these muscles are simply engaged in supporting your sound.

You don't need to do 100 crunches every morning to be able to sing, however. If you're engaging the abdominal muscles that much, you're doing it wrong. Relax, and try this:

1. Presuming nobody else is around that can cart you off to the asylum (or you're already committed and care very little about who hears you), let out a loud guttural "belly laugh." Do you feel the muscles in your abdomen contract as you do? These are the muscles in question. These are called the intercostals muscles.
2. To help you learn to voluntarily engage and control these muscles, try a sustained "hiss." No vocalization, just air. A sustained and moderately forceful hiss should engage the intercostals muscles and give you an idea as to what it should feel like to use proper breath support. Now, practice!

Music Theory: Accidentals, Half Steps & Whole Steps

Accidentals

Perhaps, in music, you've heard the words "sharp" or "flat" tossed around but don't know exactly what they mean. Sharps (♯), flats (♭), and naturals (♮) all fall under the same umbrella term of "accidentals." An accidental occurs in music when a note is written that is outside of the key signature or "home scale" of the piece. A sharp (♯) raises the pitch of a note one half step (aka semitone) while a flat (♭) lowers it a half step. A natural (♮) simply cancels or reinstates the flats or sharps of the key signature. Now, what is a half step?

Half Steps

A *semitone*, also called a *half step* or a *half tone*, is the smallest musical interval commonly used in Western tonal music. A half step creates an interval of a minor second (more on intervals in chapter 4) and is considered to be a distinctly dissonant sounding interval. Specifically, a half step refers to the interval between two adjacent notes within a 12-tone scale (C to C♯ for example, or E to E♭).

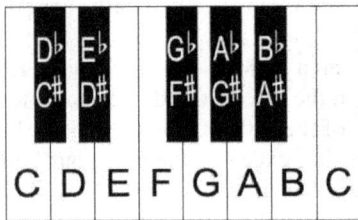

The diagram on the left shows us one octave of a piano keyboard. Count the number of keys (black and white) from the 1st 'C' to 'B.' This is the 12-tone (or chromatic) scale referred to in the above paragraph. Now, to find an example of a half step, take one note and move either left or right to the adjacent key (white or black). You move left or right depending on if you want to flatten or sharpen the note respectively. From the note 'G,' for example, to flatten it (lower it a half step) you would move to the left one key. This brings us to the black key 'G♭.' If you wanted to sharpen it (raise it a half step), you would move to the *right* to the next adjacent key. This would bring you to 'G♯.' By now, you're probably wondering why the black keys have two note names written on them. This is because those pitches have different names depending on which direction you're coming from. Let me explain. Take the pitch 'G♯' for example. If I were to add a flat to the pitch 'A' it would bring me to the same pitch, but it would be called A♭. This is called an *enharmonic*. It's the same pitch with two different names depending on the context it's in. It's like the words "naught" and "not." They sound the same, but they're spelled differently.

Whole Steps

Now, what's a whole step? Simply, a whole step is equal to 2 half steps. The interval between 'C' and 'D', for example, is a whole step. All scales are built from patterns of whole steps and half steps.

Music History: The Mass

As discussed in the previous chapter, the Catholic Church played a huge role in the development of western music.
It has stood as one of the few common factors in every period of western music since the fall of Rome and the evolution of music within the Mass is a central part of that.

Generally speaking, the music of the Mass is centered around 5 parts. Together, they constitute what is called the "Ordinary of the Mass."

Mass of St. Gregory, 1486 by the Master of the Holy Kinship

1. Kyrie ("Lord have mercy")
2. Gloria ("Glory to God in the highest")
3. Credo ("I believe in one God") aka the Nicene Creed
4. Sanctus ("Holy, Holy, Holy")
5. Agnus Dei ("Lamb of God")

Each of these components has a biblical basis that is critical to know in order to understand the importance placed on each part.

Kyrie
The Greek text "Kýrie, eléison" (pronounced "kee-ree-ay eh-leh-ee-sahn") translates to "Lord, have mercy." This phrase is used in a number of places throughout the Bible. There are many within the Old Testament (Psalm 4:2, 9:14, 25:11 121:3, Isaiah 33:2, Tobit 8:10 etc.) as well as the New Testament (Matthew 9:27, 20:30, 15:22, Mark 10:47, Luke 16:24, 17:13)

> *When he heard that it was Jesus of Nazareth, he began to shout out and say, "Jesus, Son of David, have mercy on me"* (Mark 10:47)

Gloria
The *Gloria* (pronounced "gloh-ree-ah"), or Greater Doxology, is described in the General Instruction of the Roman Missal (GIRM) as "a most ancient and venerable hymn by which the Church, gathered in the Holy Spirit, glorifies and entreats God the Father and the Lamb." To find the basis for the Gloria, check out Luke 2:14:

> *Glory to God in the highest heaven, and on earth peace among those whom he favors.* (Some translations read "peace, goodwill among people")

Credo

Latin for "I believe", the *Credo* (pronounced "kray-doh") is a statement of the basic beliefs of the Catholic Church. This comes from the Nicene Creed, originally adopted at the Council of Nicaea in 325 A.D. and updated at the Council of Constantinople in 381. Since it is quite long, however, many modern musical settings of the Mass choose not to include it.

Sanctus

Latin for "Holy", the *Sanctus* (pronounced "sAWnk-toos") is included as part of the Eucharistic Prayer (the central focus of the entire Mass where communion is prepared). The biblical basis for the first part of the *Sanctus* comes from Isaiah 6:13 where Isaiah describes a vision of the throne of God surrounded by seraphim (the highest choir of angels in the Christian tradition), which states:

> *In the year that King Uzziah died, I saw the Lord sitting on a throne, high and lofty; and the hem of his robe filled the temple, Seraphs were in attendance above him; each had six wings: with two they covered their faces, and with two they covered their feet, and with two they flew. And one called to another and said: "Holy, holy, holy is the LORD of hosts; the whole earth is full of his glory."*

Agnus Dei

Meaning "Lamb of God" in Latin, the *Agnus Dei* (pronounced Ah-nyoos Day-ee) is sung at the breaking of the Host during the Eucharistic Prayer. It is believed that the *Agnus Dei* was first introduced to the Mass in the late 7th century by Pope Sergius I. To find the biblical basis, check out John 1:29 where John the Baptist announces Christ's arrival at the River Jordan:

> *The next day he saw Jesus coming toward him and declared, "Here is the Lamb of God who takes away the sins of the world! (John 1:29)*

Baptism of Christ, ca. 1580 by Jacopo Tintoretto

14

Sight-Reading: adding Fa and Sol

In this chapter, we're going to continue to expand on our knowledge and use of solfège by adding the next two syllables, "fa" and "sol," which represent the 4th and 5th notes of the major scale respectively. First, recall our solfège diagram in C major:

Do Re Mi Fa Sol La Ti Do

Now, let's try some examples using "fa" (pronounced "fah" as in father) and "sol" (pronounced like "soul").

1.

Do Re Mi Re   Mi Fa Sol   Sol Fa Mi Re   Do Do Do

2.

Do Re Re Mi   Do Mi Re Mi   Fa Fa Sol Sol   Fa Mi Re Do

3.

Do Mi Re Fa   Mi Sol Fa Mi   Re Re Do   Do Re Mi Do

4.

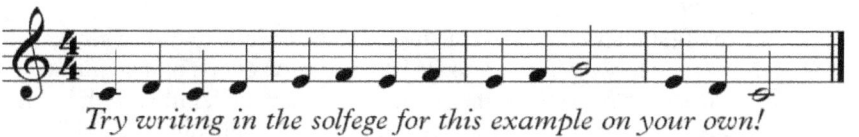

Try writing in the solfege for this example on your own!

5.

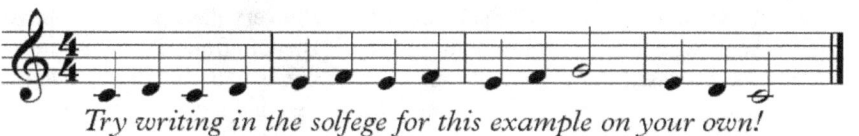

Try writing in the solfege for this example on your own!

Performance: Kyrie XI (Orbis Factor)

The *Kyriale* is a collection of 18 chant settings for the Ordinary of the Mass. The *Kyriale* is often printed by itself as a separate book by the monks of Solesmes Abbey, but is also included in other liturgical texts such as the *Graduale Romanum* and *Liber Usualis*. The *Kyrie* from Mass XI (*Missa Orbis Factor*) is perhaps the most popular *Kyrie* of the *Kyriale*. *Kyrie XI* is almost exclusively notated using neumatic (chant) notation (see chapter 2). Here, however, it has been translated into modern notation for your convenience. Check it out below:

NOTE

- *Kyrie XI* makes use of a type of rhythm called a "triplet." You can see on beat 4 of measure 2. It looks like the figure on the right. This mechanism allows you to have three even notes over one beat instead of 2 or 4. You can simply count these as "tri-pl-et." For example, measure 2-3 would be counted like this: "ti-ki, ti-ki, ti-ki, tri-pl-et, ti-ki, ta-ah."
- Notice that above measures 1,4,7 and 10 there are marks that read as "3x" or "2x." This simply indicates how many times that particular section is to be sung.
- In the first interval, we see the use of an accidental; B flat. This makes the first two intervals (from A to B flat back to A) only a half step instead of a whole step. This is the same sound as you may be familiar with in the theme from the movie *Jaws*. "duh duh duh duh duh duh duh duh"

TIPS

- If you don't happen to speak ancient Greek every day, you might have an issue with pronunciation with this piece. Be not afraid, I've got your back. As discussed in the previous chapter, we can usually break down any word into the 5 Latin Vowels to make them more conducive to singing. In this case, we would sing the words: "Kee-ree-eh eh-leh-ee-sahn, Kree-steh eh-leh-ee-sahn." Try it!

Chapter 4

Technique: Diction

We've already discussed the Five Latin Vowels, the five "keys to tone." They are one of the most fundamental elements of choral diction. When we sing, the sound of the sung language (English or otherwise) is different than the spoken language. While some of the things we are asked to do with diction may sound unusual from your perspective, certain purities and exaggerations must be observed for the sound to be correct by the time it melds with the other voices and reaches the ears of the audience.

Diphthongs

Pronounced "DIF-thong," and also known as a *gliding vowel*, a diphthong refers to two adjacent vowel sounds that occur within the same syllable. When we sing, we place the emphasis on the first of the two vowel sounds. The second vowel sound should simply be allowed to happen naturally at the very end. Here are some examples:

Sounds Like	Examples
ah:ee	Price, my, high, flight, mice
ah:oo	Mouth, now, trout
eh:ee	Face, date, day, they grey, pain, reign
oh:ee	Choice, boy, hoist
oh:oo	Goat, toe, tow, soul, rope, cold

Triphthongs

Similar to the diphthong, the triphthong (pronounced "TRIF-thong") is a combination of vowel sounds within a single syllable. We also treat them in much the same way as a diphthong. You stress the first of the three vowel sounds, allowing what follows to occur naturally and with minimal stress. Here are some examples of triphthongs:

Sounds Like	Examples
ah:oo:wah	Hour, flower, power
ah:ee:wah	Fire, pyre, choir

Consonants

With all this discussion of vowels, we would be amiss not to cover the other side of the coin; consonants. Here are a few tips to consider with consonants:

1. As a general rule, sung consonants require more energy behind them in order to be audibly distinct than when they are simply spoken. We often use the phrase "spitting the consonants out" to illustrate this concept. This is particularly true of *plosive consonants* (p,q,b,t,d,c,k,g).

2. The letter "r" should never be sung through (resulting in a rather unpleasant "er" sound). Instead, it is typical for the "r" to be *flipped*. This action is similar to a *trilled* or "rolled r" but only involves one brief interruption of airflow. The 'r' sound may also be eliminated altogether.

3. Ending consonants that are followed immediately by another word without a rest in between are typically attached to the first syllable of the next word.

4. Have a word that ends on a plosive consonant? Try adding a brief, almost inaudible "ah" after the consonant for clarity.

17

Music Theory: Basic Intervals

We've already talked about our two most basic intervals in music, the half step and the whole step. All music is composed of steps and leaps. We've covered the steps, so let's look at the leaps.

The term *interval* simply refers to the distance between two pitches. To identify the quality of the interval, count the number of lines and spaces between the two notes in question. Let's look at the basic intervals, the intervals of the major scale:

Major 2nd   Major 3rd   Perfect 4th   Perfect 5th   Major 6th   Major 7th   Octave

Whether ascending or descending, the interval is the same. Here are some songs you can use to recognize each interval:

Interval	Ascending	Descending
M2	Silent Night	The First Noel
M3	Kum Ba Yah	Swing Low Sweet Chariot
P4	Amazing Grace	Oh, Come All ye Faithful
P5	Twinkle, Twinkle	Flintstones
M6	It Came Upon a Midnight Clear	Nobody Knows the Trouble I've Seen
M7	Superman	I Love You (Cole Porter)
Octave	Somewhere Over the Rainbow	There's No Business Like Show Business (Notes 2-3)

Music Theory: Advanced Intervals

Odds are, if you don't see an accidental before the note, you're dealing with one of the intervals listed above. But what if there IS an accidental? Well, you might have one of the intervals listed below (The enharmonics are listed for you):

Minor 2nd   Minor 3rd   Tritone   Minor 6th   Minor 7th

Here are some recognizable songs to help you identify these advanced intervals:

Interval	Ascending	Descending
m2	Jaws	Joy to the World
m3	Greensleeves	Frosty the Snowman
TT	The Simpsons	Blue Seven (Sonny Rollins)
m6	Go Down Moses	Love Story Theme
m7	There's a Place for Us (West Side Story)	Watermelon Man (H. Hancock)

Music History: Carols

A carol is a festive song. Most are religious, but carols are not necessarily connected with church worship as they tend to be of a dance-like or popular nature. Today, the common repertoire of carols is dominated by the Christmas carol, though there are Advent carols, and some Easter carols as well.

The word "carol" comes from the French *carole*, defined as a social dance of the 12th and 13th centuries, common in both courtly and popular society and danced to refrain songs sung by a soloist on the verses alternating with the full group (chorus) singing the refrain. Similarly a carol is typically identified by its refrain – verse structure, though some are more complex.

Carols fell into a steep decline following the Protestant Reformation (1517-1648) due to the Calvinist approach of abolishing "nonessential" practices that could be associated with Catholicism. The 19th century, however, saw a revival in the writing of carols led by composers such as Lowell Mason and Arthur Sullivan, though the carol never regained its former popularity.

Κάλαντα by Nikiphoros Lytras (1832-1904)

Sight-Reading: Adding La and Ti

In this chapter, we're going to continue to expand on our knowledge and use of solfège by adding the last two standard syllables, "la" and "ti," which represent the 6th and 7th notes of the major scale respectively. First, recall our solfège diagram in C major:

Do Re Mi Fa Sol La Ti Do

Now, let's try some examples using "la" (pronounced "lah" as in laud) and "ti" (pronounced like "tea"). Note that only some of the solfège is provided for you:

Performance: The First Noel

The First Noel (sometimes written The First Noël or The First Nowell) is an English carol. The word *Noel* comes from the French *Noël* meaning Christmas. It was first published in *Carols Ancient and Modern* arranged by Davies Gilbert and edited by Williams Sandys. The typical arrangement performed today is the 1871 four-part hymn arrangement by English composer John Stainer.

NOTE

- The First Noel contains a common pronunciation pitfall. The word "the" can be pronounced two different ways, and they are not interchangeable. When *the* precedes a word that begins with a consonant, it is pronounced "thuh." When *the* precedes a word that begins with a vowel, it is pronounced "thee." The first part of the song, then, would be pronounced "*thuh* first Noel *thee* angel did say…"

- Another very common pronunciation pitfall is the last word of the refrain: *Israel*. In America, we have often bastardized the pronunciation to "Iz-rye-el." This is simply not correct. The pronunciation of the word does vary, however, depending on whether you are singing in Latin or English. If you are singing in Latin, the word is pronounced "Eez-rah-el." However, with The First Noel being in English, the word should be pronounced "Iz-ray-el."

TIP

- Try singing *The First Noel* on solfège first!

Chapter 5

Technique: Marking your Music

As you sit through a rehearsal, you will be given instructions by your director that would best be remembered by marking it in your music. This is a great way to bring attention to what you've learned and what you should practice.

Always use a pencil, not a pen. Directions can change, but a pen is permanent. Using a pen can make it very difficult to indicate further changes to your music. For your benefit and the benefit of those who use the same copy of music after you, always use a pencil.

The method of choral shorthand is an individual matter. Whatever method you have used, or care to use, is fine – so long as it is meaningful to you. Here are some example notations that you might find helpful.

	WATCH!		TEMPO CONTROL!
(ƒ) (ppp)	Follow dynamics		*Forte* release
p	*Piano* release		Circle any pitch where error has been made.
	Listen! Arrow to another part	↓ 1 2 3 4	Cut-off on, for ex., the 4th beat.
	Hold note and sustain to release		Placement of final consonant
	No accent.		Stress.
	Crescendo. Increase dynamic		*Decrescendo.* Decrease dynamic
, ✓	Breathing marks.		Hold. *Fermata.*

Of course, in addition to these markings, you might write in your counts or solfège. However you mark your music, it must be distinct, important, and noticeable. You can scribble on your music to your heart's content but, if it isn't something you notice or practice, it's wasted effort.

Music Theory: Dynamics

Dynamics indicate the volume of a particular note or section of music. The two most basic dynamics are *piano* (*p*) meaning "soft," and *forte* (*f*) meaning "loud." Beyond that, however, are more subtle degrees of loudness and softness. We have *mezzo-piano* (*mp*) meaning "moderately soft, and *mezzo-forte* (*mf*) meaning "moderately loud." Beyond that we have, on the more extreme ends of the spectrum, *pianissimo* (*pp*) meaning "very soft," and *fortissimo* (*ff*) meaning "very loud." See the chart below for examples:

DYNAMIC	MEANING	VOCAL EXAMPLE
ppp	*Pianississimo* – "very very soft"	Whisper
pp	*Pianissimo* – "very soft"	Almost a whisper
p	*Piano* – "soft"	Softer than speaking voice
mp	*Mezzo-piano*– "moderately soft"	Speaking voice
mf	*Mezzo-forte*– "moderately loud"	Speaking voice
f	*Forte* – "loud"	Louder than speaking voice
ff	*Fortissimo* – "very loud"	Speaking loudly
fff	*Fortississimo* – "very very loud"	Yelling

Music Theory: Road Maps

Composers will often use symbols to indicate points in music to jump to and from Let's take a look at some of the more basic symbols.

Repeat Sign – this indicates a section of the music that is to be performed again. When it appears alone, return to the beginning of the music. If it appears as the second of a pair, repeat only the section within the two repeat signs.

***Dal segno* (D.S.)** - Sing until you reach the words *dal segno* or *D.S.* and return to the *sign* indicated on the left.

da capo(D.C.)   Return to the beginning of the music.

al fine   You will most likely see this indication as part of a *D.C. al fine* or *D.S. al fine*. After you make the jump to the beginning or the sign, sing until you reach the word *fine* (pronounced "fee-neh").

al coda – similarly to *al fine*, *al coda* will be found as part of a *D.C.* or *D.S.*, at which point you make the jump and sing until you see the *coda* sign (seen on the left) and jump to the coda section, following directions from there.

Music History: Christian Hymnody

The tradition of Christian hymnody goes back as far as the Christian faith itself. The earliest hymns we know of were first mentioned by St. Paul in his letters circa 65 AD. As discussed in previous chapters, the church was the primary force in the development of music in the western world for centuries and, as such, the Christian hymn tradition was a big part of that. Until the Protestant Reformation (1517-1648), that tradition rested almost exclusively in the hands of the Catholic Church, which introduced polyphony, major and minor keys, four-part vocal harmony, and the use of organ and choir to lead the music in worship.

The Protestant Reformation, however, brought about two highly conflicting perspectives on hymnody. As discussed in Chapter 4, the Calvinists and other more radical reformers had much more restrictive views on the incorporation of music into worship as well as anything else that could be considered remotely Catholic in origin. As a result, most hymns were banned by Calvinists and similar sects in favor of a tradition called *exclusive psalmody*, in which the only singing permitted in worship is directly taken from the book of Psalms in the Bible.

Martin Luther, however, held no such radical views on Christian hymnody. Quite the opposite, Luther and his followers utilized hymnody as a means of teaching the tenets of their faith.

Certainly the development of Christian hymnody didn't end with the Protestant Reformation, however. Every generation has something to add to this, one of the oldest musical traditions. The Methodist Revival of the 18th century, the American slavery period, the Second Great Awakening (1790-1840), along with every generation of people has had their mark to add on the tradition. Today, many churches opt to use contemporary music for worship influenced by popular styles such as jazz, R&B, and rock and roll. This practice began in the 1960s but didn't become truly popular until the 1970s. Many American churches today with primarily African-American congregations tend toward gospel style music in their worship. All this is said to illustrate a point; Christian hymnody is an ever-evolving organic tradition. Unlike many subjects of historical study, Christian hymnody is not solely in the past. It is also very much alive in the present, and will continue to be here in the future, if only a little different.

As St. Thomas Aquinas once described it; "A hymn is the praise of God with song; a song is the exultation of the mind dwelling on eternal things, bursting forth in the voice."

Sight-Reading: Putting it all together

By now, we have looked through all of the basic principles necessary to sight-read in our church choir. There are certainly many more principles you can learn and entire libraries of books for you to absorb but, by this point, you should have mastered the basic tools you need to survive. Now, let's put it all together in a step by step guide to reading a new piece of music that your director hands you.

1. Read the title of the piece. This might seem like a "no-brainer" kind of step, but you may be surprised to find out how much the title alone will help you in defining the mood of the piece. One only needs to hear Beethoven's *Moonlight Sonata* in the original tempo (about twice as fast as you've ever heard it) before a publisher decided on the title to see how much a few words can influence the performance of a piece.
2. Look for road maps and take note of them. Where are the jumps in this piece?
3. Find 'Do' using the *Rule of Fa & Ti:*
    > **If the key signature is in flats, find the second to last flat, that note is 'Do.' If the key signature is in sharps, take the last sharp and raise it one half step to find 'Do.'**
4. Find your voice part and look ahead. Which line is yours?
5. Look for changes. Does the meter signature change? What about the key?
6. Find the challenges. Skip over the parts that look easy and find the parts that look more challenging. Mentally rehearse these a few times so that you will be ready when you get to them.
7. Look over the text.
8. Read through the beginning.
9. Read the very last line.
10. Read the beginning again.
11. Breathe, and look ahead. Try not to give up or get too frustrated. Sight-reading takes time. Go slowly at first be sure to listen to those around you. Remember that you're part of a group, not just an individual.
12. Have fun!

15th century painting by Jan van Eyck

Performance: Amazing Grace

Amazing Grace is perhaps the most recognizable Christian hymns in the English speaking world today. The text was written sometime in the 18th century by John Newton, an Anglican cleric, and was first published in 1779. The melody, "New Britain" was first published in 1829 by Charles H. Spillman and Benjamin Shaw, though it is not attributed to any particular composer. The melody and text were first combined into the hymn we know today by William Walker in 1835.

Using the steps outlined in the previous section, try sight-reading *Amazing Grace.*

TIPS

- Try singing *Amazing Grace* on solfège. (Done for you below)
- Having trouble with the triplets? Don't forget to use the counting system outlined in previous chapters.
- Notice that the notes on "me" and "see" are tied across a barline. These ties add duration by combining note values. In both of these cases we have a dotted half note (3 beats) tied to a half note (2 beats) meaning that both of these notes are 5 beats long. Make sure you hold them out for their full value!

Be sure to check out the pages that follow. There you will find such useful tools as a list of common musical terms and their definitions and a suggested listening list to help you continue on your journey into sacred choral music.

Thank you for choosing *Quintessential Choir: Church Choir Edition.* Happy learning and don't forget to have fun!

List of Musical Terms

Term	Definition
Accelerando	Gradually faster
Adagio	Slowly
Allargando	Slowing down, broadly
Allegro	Fast
Andante	Moderately slowly
A tempo	Back to the original tempo
Brio	Fire
Cantabile	Singing style
Con	With
Crescendo	Getting louder
Da capo	Return to the beginning
Dal segno	Return to the sign
Decrescendo	Getting softer
Diminuendo	Getting softer
Dolce	Sweetly
Fermata	Hold at will
Forte	Loudly
Fortissimo	Very loudly
Fozando	With force
Fuoco	Fire
Giocoso	Playfully
Grave	Slowly
Larghetto	Slowly
Legato	Smoothly connected
Lento	Slowly
Maestoso	Majestically, stately
Marcato	Accented
Meno	Less
Meno mosso	Less movement
Mezzo	Half
Moderato	Moderately
Molto	Much
Non troppo	Not too much
Pianissimo	Very softly
Piu	More

Piu mosso	More movement
Poco	Little
Presto	Very fast
Rallentando	Gradually slower
Ritardando	Gradually slower
Sempre	Always
Senza	Without
Sforzando	Accented
Simile	Similar
Sostenuto	Sustained
Sotto voce	Soft voice
Staccato	Detached
Subito	Suddenly
Tempo	Time/speed
Tenuto	Held longer
Tranquillo	Tranquilly
Troppo	Too much
Vivace	Very fast
Vivo	Lively

Suggested Listening List

The greatest tool you have available to you as an aspiring musician is listening. Go out and find recordings of choirs that you like and think about what makes them so appealing to you. Are these aspects something that you can incorporate into your own music making? The greatest authors of the world didn't get to where they are by never reading a book and you, as an advocate of the musical arts, haven't gotten to where you are without listening a great deal to music over the years. Continue that practice and refine it. You'll become a better musician for it. Here's a list to get you started.

Composer	Work
Allegri	Miserere
Bach	Mass in B minor
Bach	St. Matthew Passion
Bach	St. John Passion
Beethoven	Missa Solemnis
Brahms	Ein Deutsches Requiem
Britten	War Requiem
Bruckner	Mass No. 2 in E minor
Elgar	The Dream of Gerontius
Faure	Requiem
Handel	Messiah
Handel	Coronation Anthems
Haydn	Missa in Angustiis 'Nelson Mass'
Hayden	The Creation
Mahler	Symphony No.8 Symphony of a Thousand'
Mendelssohn	Elijah
Monteverdi	Vespers of 1610
Mozart	Requiem
Mozart	Mass in C mino
Orff	Carmina Burana
Poulenc	Gloria
Tallis	Spem in alium
Vaughan Williams	Serenade to Music
Verdi	Reqiuem
Vivaldi	Gloria

www.ingramcontent.com/pod-product-compliance
Lightning Source LLC
Chambersburg PA
CBHW031531040426
42445CB00009B/486